TRADITIONAL CHINESE CUT-PAPER DESIGNS

COLLECTED AND EDITED BY
BERND MELCHERS

DOVER PUBLICATIONS, INC.
NEW YORK

To REINHOLD GRIMM
in remembrance of our years together in China

Published in Canada by General Publishing Company, Ltd., 30 Lesmill Road, Don Mills, Toronto, Ontario.

Published in the United Kingdom by Constable and Company, Ltd., 10 Orange Street, London WC2H 7EG.

This Dover edition, first published in 1978, is an unabridged republication of the work originally published by Hugo Bruckmann, Munich, in 1921, with the title *Chinesische Schattenschnitte: ein Bilderbuch.* The German text has been replaced by a new English translation specially prepared for the present edition by Stanley Appelbaum. The original edition was printed in a variety of colors.

International Standard Book Number:
0-486-23581-5
Library of Congress Catalog Card Number:
77-88654

Manufactured in the United States of America
Dover Publications, Inc.
180 Varick Street
New York, N.Y. 10014

INTRODUCTION

Although the pictures in the present volume are folk art of the simplest kind, they are an echo of Chinese high art. The poorest people buy these brightly colored images for a fraction of a penny and decorate their paper lanterns with them. Yet if you leaf through Chinese books about painting, you will recognize the models for these cut-paper designs among the renderings of the works of the most famous masters. Nevertheless, no matter how closely the cut-paper designs follow those renderings—and at first glance it appears that they merely repeat them line by line—they are still art works in their own right, cut by the hands of artists.

To be sure, the method of their production is quite mechanical. About six layers of thin paper, colored on one side, are stacked up and firmly attached to an already existing cutout by means of little pegs which the worker himself rolls out of tissue paper. Then he cuts out the contours and the larger inner surfaces with a pair of those thick, clumsy shears which are capable of the finest work when placed in the slender, incredibly quick hands of the Chinese. Most of the inner surfaces and lines, however, are more punched out than cut out, and the tools in this case are the small knives used in making woodcuts.

Moreover, if you could catch a glimpse of the man who made most of the cutouts in this collection—dirty and scrawny, sitting on a street corner—if you were to see a number of his earliest designs, only a few of which have been included here, you would scarcely venture to call him an artist. And yet he was one. For even those first designs, not to mention the later ones, acquire a life of their own when used as they were meant to be–when held up against the light as shadow pictures—a life that has too often been lost in those constantly copied and repeated renderings of paintings.

A comparison of his products with those of a second design cutter shows that the artistic effect of these cutouts is far from a matter of course. This second worker created the

animals on pages 5, 17, 24 and 25, everything on page 30, the cat on page 46, pages 47, 50 and 51, the plant and the deer on page 59, the pine branch on page 60 and the man with the umbrella on page 40 struggling forward against rain and wind. Of course, most of these were subsequently recut, and thus improved, by the first-mentioned artist. In their original form these, and the many others not reproduced here, appeared at first glance much stronger artistically than the others. The explanation was easily found: they were based on artistically superior models, being almost exclusively taken from the best-known instruction book for painting, the *Jie Tsi Yuan,* the textbook of the "Mustardseed Garden." But if these cutouts are held against the light alongside those of the seemingly far cruder ones of the first artist, they prove to be unclear, confused and ineffective, whereas the others are filled with warm life. One man had only traced the model renderings and cut them out without understanding the demands of their new purpose. But that first man created something artistically new by translating the lines into surfaces and at the same time simplifying his models with an eye to the new purpose and the altered mode of production.

It was in the year 1913 that Georg Walter, my co-worker at the time, discovered the artist on one of the streets of a suburb of Tsinan, capital of Shantung and terminus of the railroad that leads from Tsingtao to the interior. [The province of Shantung was then a German sphere of influence.—*Translator*.] He immediately brought him along to our farm, and with joy and amazement we extracted the bright pictures from the portfolios—stiff with dirt—in which they were kept for sale. Unfortunately Georg Walter was not able to enjoy them long. He was one of the first to fall at his advanced post near Tsingtao while trying to bring aid to a wounded man in his unit. [At the outset of World War I in August 1914 the Japanese and British attacked the German holdings in China.—*Translator*.]

Only a few of those earliest cutouts are reproduced here, including the theatrical figures on pages 32, 33, 38, 39 and 49. Most of them were too crude in comparison with the later ones, although they were often jollier and closer to folk art than many of the others. They had to be

omitted because only a little over a third of the whole collection could find a place in the present volume.

It is hard to say where the models for all these cutouts came from—surely from many different sources, their styles are so divergent. Some of them are strongly reminiscent of metalwork, such as the lioness with the cub on page 18, the fish on pages 10 and 43 and the circular ornament on page 52. Similar in treatment are the swordsmen on pages 38 and 39, especially the smaller one, and the unusually cut fisherman on page 12, who in turn is both peculiarly contrasted to, and yet related to, the beggar on page 6, who represents one of the Eight Immortals.

Quite different in concept are most of the representations of branches and flowers and the large figures on pages 62 and 63, gate-keepers who ward off evil spirits. Still different are the written characters, rendered in broad, strong forms meant to be read from a distance, such as the two versions of the character *fu,* "happiness, prosperity," on pages 60 and 61. The various ornamental pieces were clearly based

on a different art form, probably on weaving and embroidery patterns. As far as I know, the large cutouts of this type are not used on lamps, but for decorating the tissue-paper bases, coffers, litters and chests that are burned at funerals along with various figures of animals and people to accompany the deceased on his journey.

In the course of time new pictures were constantly added to the collection until finally no more were to be found. Then one day the artist brought me tracings from some book and asked whether he should make me cutouts from them. They were figures drawn in thin, weak lines in an over-refined and fairly boring manner. I barely recognized them when they were presented to me as cutouts filled with a new vitality. They are reproduced on pages 24, 25, 26, 54 and 55 (right-hand figure). Here the cutout artist's own contribution can be directly observed, and I regret that I could not place the model images alongside the cutouts in this book to show how different and how much more dramatic the latter are. It was also in this last period that the artist produced many of the small individual figures on pages 41, 52 and 64, the classroom group on page 45, the fish on page 43 and finally (page 48) K'wei Hsing, one of the patron gods of literature, who is represented as a devil through a truly Chinese play on words.

It was not easy to induce our eccentric artist to work; he often stayed away for months at a time. Finally he disappeared altogether. His brother had become an officer somewhere or other, and now the whole family went to join him so that he could support them.

I have no knowledge of cutouts of this quality from places other than Tsinan, but this is no proof that they are not found elsewhere. After all, very few people pay any attention to minor arts of this type, especially when, like these pictures, they are literally to be found on the street. Naturally, the Chinese do not collect this sort of thing, and Europeans all too often pass by even major works of art without seeing them. I obtained similar cutouts, which presuppose the same traditions, only from Tientsin, but they were poorly cut and made of ugly colored paper of the European variety.

In his *Pekinger Volkskunde* (Ethnography of Peking), Grube has published cut-paper designs that are used for a different purpose. Cut from the thinnest tissue paper, they are embroidery patterns which the women place directly onto the material and sew over. To suit the different purpose, the method of cutting is also different. The individual forms must be worked out in much greater detail and perhaps for that reason often appear dull and inartistic, especially

the human and animal figures. On the other hand, the grouping and dovetailing of branches and tendrils within a given space is in general surprisingly delightful, as in the patterns for embroidered shoes that I also found in Tsinan.

The arrangement of the cutouts in this volume is arbitrary, but this corresponds to the popular national custom of grouping these pictures in a cheerful confusion. Unfortunately, this variegation of color is not so conspicuous in the present volume because the printing process allowed the use of only one color per page. [This 1978 edition is in black ink only.—*Translator*.]

Yet it is hoped that, even so, these pictures will give joy to many people and tell them in shadow play about the life of a distant Chinese city.

DR. BERND MELCHERS

Bremen, November 12, 1920

34

35

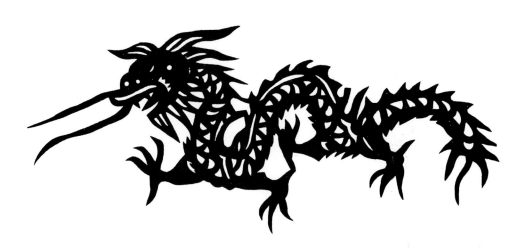

48